Wise Words
to Trust

Words of wisdom from the
Book of Proverbs

Carine Mackenzie
Illustrated by Helen Smith

The fear of the LORD
is the beginning of
knowledge; but fools
despise wisdom and
instruction.
Proverbs 1:7

He who keeps
instruction is in the
way of life,
but he who refuses
correction goes astray.
Proverbs 10:17

**He who oppresses the poor reproaches his Maker, but he who honours him has mercy on the needy.
Proverbs 14:31**

Many children in our world are hungry and sick because of the greed and cruelty of wicked men. Those who love and honour God should show kindness to the poor and give whenever they are able. Showing kindness to a needy person who follows Jesus, is like showing kindness to Jesus himself.

PRAYER

Dear Lord God, so many children in the world are hungry. I cannot do very much to help them, but do not let me forget them. Help me to do what I can, for your sake. Amen.

The name of the LORD is a strong tower, the righteous run to it and are safe.
Proverbs 18:10

These children are running together away from the rain. They need shelter. The tower in the park looks like a good place to go. It's a strong, safe place. God is a shelter and a safe place for his people. God's name tells us what he is like. He is faithful, powerful, merciful and wise. So we can safely trust in him at all times.

PRAYER

Lord, you are strong and faithful and wise. Thank you that I can trust in you for safety and help, through the Lord Jesus Christ. Amen.

Apply your heart to instruction and your ears to words of knowledge.
Proverbs 23:12

These children are listening intently to their teacher. The wise person is always eager to learn from others but especially from the greatest Teacher, the Lord Jesus Christ whose teaching we read in the Bible.

PRAYER

Lord, thank you for my teachers and everyone who helps me to learn. Help me to listen carefully to your Word when it is read and preached. You are the best teacher. Amen.

A prudent man foresees evil and hides himself.
Proverbs 27:12

The boys notice that the mist is rolling in. If they continue on the path they may walk into danger. It would be better to shelter in the rocks till conditions improve. If we are wise we will keep away from activities or places that will lead us into sin.

PRAYER

Oh Lord, please keep me from danger and temptation and sin. Help me to turn away from evil and to obey your commands. Amen.

He who is of a proud heart stirs up strife, but he who trusts in the LORD will be prospered.
Proverbs 28:25

The boy is proud and greedy and is causing a quarrel with his sister. How much happier they would both be if he showed humility and kindness. True contentment comes from God. It is a great gift.

Prayer

Dear Lord, when I feel proud and nasty, help me to stop and think of you. Help me to trust in you all the time, and to show love to my friends and family. Amen.

He who disdains instruction despises his own soul, but he who heeds rebuke gets understanding.
Proverbs 15:32

The fruit of the
righteous is a tree
of life, and he who
wins souls is wise.
Proverbs 11:30

Do not withhold good from those to whom it is due, when it is in the power of your hand to do so.
Proverbs 3:27

The bigger boy has stopped to help the younger one who has fallen off his bicycle. Jesus was always helping others. He wants us to be like him. He wants us to trust in him. Then we will be truly wise.

PRAYER

Lord, please help me to be more like Jesus who was always helping others. I confess that I am often selfish and want to do what pleases me. Help me to do what is pleasing to you. Amen.

Pleasant words are like a honeycomb, sweetness to the soul and health to the bones.
Proverbs 16:24

When you get hurt, you want to run to mum or dad for comfort. Their kind words reassure you and help you to feel better. God's Word is the best comfort when we are in trouble.

PRAYER

Lord, your Word is the best comfort when I am in trouble. Help me to read it and remember it and think about it. May my words always be true and pleasing to you. Amen.

**Whoever robs his father or mother, and says "It is no transgression," the same is companion to a destroyer.
Proverbs 28:24**

The boy is stealing from his mother's purse when she is not looking. He might say "It's all right. It is really mine too." God says that is terribly wrong.

PRAYER

Oh Lord, I often do things that are wrong. Help me to be honest and upright when I am at home, at school, in the shops, in church and everywhere I go. You see everything I do. Amen.

The way of a fool
is right in his own
eyes, but a wise man
is he who listens to
counsel.
Proverbs 12:15

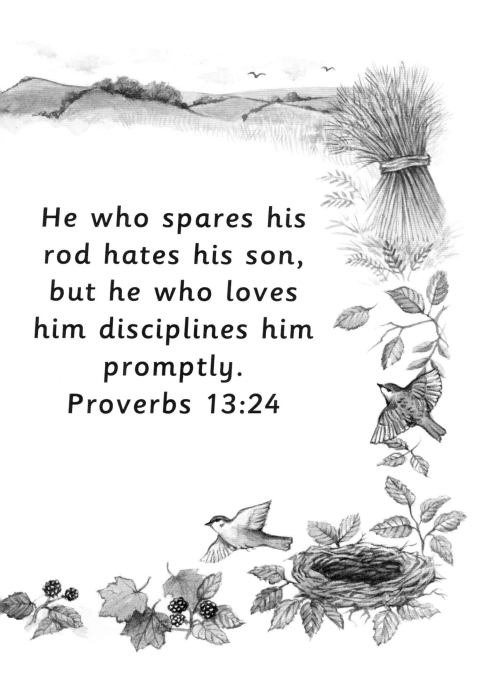

He who spares his
rod hates his son,
but he who loves
him disciplines him
promptly.
Proverbs 13:24

Themes in this book:

Comfort: Page 18
Discipline: Page 14, 23
Kindness: 4, 16
Obedience: Page 3, 12, 20
Safety: Page 6
Wisdom: Page 2, 8, 10, 15, 22

Themes of other books in the series:

Wise Words to Obey, ISBN 978-1-84550-431-1
Commitment, forgiveness, friendship,
good news, obedience and wisdom.

Wise Words to Follow, ISBN 978-1-84550-430-4
Caring, God's blessing, guidance, listening and
learning, obedience, rest and refreshment.